# THIS LOG BELONGS TO

---

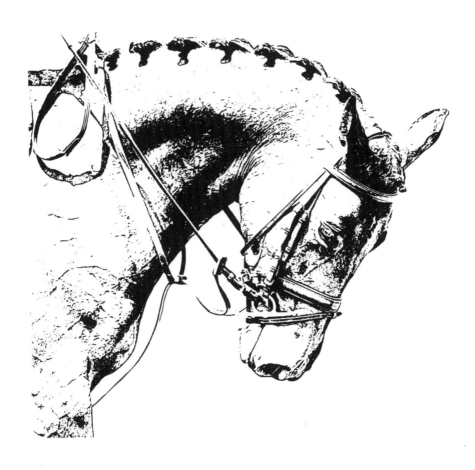

# NOTES

# Horse Show Log

Date

Venue

Event

Class

Horse(s)

Results

Notes

# Horse Show Log

Date

Venue

Event

Class

Horse(s)

Results

Notes

# Horse Show Log

Date

Venue

Event

Class

Horse(s)

Results

Notes

# Horse Show Log

Date

Venue

Event

Class

Horse(s)

Results

Notes

# HORSE SHOW LOG

Date

Venue

Event

Class

Horse(s)

Results

Notes

# HORSE SHOW LOG

Date

Venue

Event

Class

Horse(s)

Results

Notes

# Horse Show Log

Date

Venue

Event

Class

Horse(s)

Results

Notes

# Horse Show Log

Date

Venue

Event

Class

Horse(s)

Results

Notes

# Horse Show Log

Date

Venue

Event

Class

Horse(s)

Results

Notes

# HORSE SHOW LOG

Date

Venue

Event

Class

Horse(s)


Results



Notes

# Horse Show Log

Date

Venue

Event

Class

Horse(s)

Results

Notes

# HORSE SHOW LOG

Date

Venue

Event

Class

Horse(s)

Results

Notes

# Horse Show Log

Date

Venue

Event

Class

Horse(s)

Results

Notes

# HORSE SHOW LOG

Date

Venue

Event

Class

Horse(s)

Results

Notes

# Horse Show Log

Date

Venue

Event

Class

Horse(s)

Results

Notes

# Horse Show Log

Date

Venue

Event

Class

Horse(s)

Results

Notes

# Horse Show Log

Date

Venue

Event

Class

Horse(s)

Results

Notes

# HORSE SHOW LOG

Date

Venue

Event

Class

Horse(s)

Results

Notes

# Horse Show Log

Date

Venue

Event

Class

Horse(s)

Results

Notes

# HORSE SHOW LOG

Date

Venue

Event

Class

Horse(s)

Results

Notes

# Horse Show Log

Date

Venue

Event

Class

Horse(s)

Results

Notes

# HORSE SHOW LOG

Date

Venue

Event

Class

Horse(s)

Results

Notes

# Horse Show Log

Date

Venue

Event

Class

Horse(s)

Results

Notes

# HORSE SHOW LOG

Date

Venue

Event

Class

Horse(s)

Results

Notes

# Horse Show Log

Date

Venue

Event

Class

Horse(s)


Results



Notes

# HORSE SHOW LOG

Date

Venue

Event

Class

Horse(s)


Results



Notes

# Horse Show Log

Date

_____

Venue

_____

Event

_____

Class

_____

Horse(s)

_____

_____

Results

_____

_____

_____

Notes

_____

_____

_____

_____

_____

_____

_____

# HORSE SHOW LOG

Date

Venue

Event

Class

Horse(s)

Results

Notes

# HORSE SHOW LOG

Date

Venue

Event

Class

Horse(s)

Results

Notes

# HORSE SHOW LOG

Date

Venue

Event

Class

Horse(s)

Results

Notes

# HORSE SHOW LOG

Date

Venue

Event

Class

Horse(s)

Results

Notes

# Horse Show Log

Date

Venue

Event

Class

Horse(s)

Results

Notes

# Horse Show Log

Date

Venue

Event

Class

Horse(s)

Results

Notes

# Horse Show Log

Date

Venue

Event

Class

Horse(s)

Results

Notes

# Horse Show Log

Date

Venue

Event

Class

Horse(s)

Results

Notes

# HORSE SHOW LOG

Date

Venue

Event

Class

Horse(s)

Results

Notes

# Horse Show Log

Date

Venue

Event

Class

Horse(s)

Results

Notes

# Horse Show Log

Date

Venue

Event

Class

Horse(s)

Results

Notes

# Horse Show Log

Date

Venue

Event

Class

Horse(s)

Results

Notes

# HORSE SHOW LOG

Date
_____

Venue
_____

Event
_____

Class
_____

Horse(s)
_____

_____

Results
_____

_____

_____

Notes
_____

_____

_____

_____

_____

_____

_____

_____

_____

# Horse Show Log

Date

Venue

Event

Class

Horse(s)

Results

Notes

# HORSE SHOW LOG

Date

Venue

Event

Class

Horse(s)

Results

Notes

# Horse Show Log

Date

Venue

Event

Class

Horse(s)

Results

Notes

# HORSE SHOW LOG

Date

Venue

Event

Class

Horse(s)

Results

Notes

# Horse Show Log

Date

Venue

Event

Class

Horse(s)

Results

Notes

# HORSE SHOW LOG

Date

Venue

Event

Class

Horse(s)

Results

Notes

# Horse Show Log

Date

Venue

Event

Class

Horse(s)

Results

Notes

# HORSE SHOW LOG

Date

Venue

Event

Class

Horse(s)

Results

Notes

# Horse Show Log

Date

Venue

Event

Class

Horse(s)

Results

Notes

# HORSE SHOW LOG

Date

Venue

Event

Class

Horse(s)


Results



Notes

# Horse Show Log

Date

Venue

Event

Class

Horse(s)

Results

Notes

# HORSE SHOW LOG

Date

Venue

Event

Class

Horse(s)

Results

Notes

# Horse Show Log

Date

Venue

Event

Class

Horse(s)

Results

Notes

# HORSE SHOW LOG

Date

Venue

Event

Class

Horse(s)

Results

Notes

# Horse Show Log

Date

Venue

Event

Class

Horse(s)

Results

Notes

# Horse Show Log

Date

Venue

Event

Class

Horse(s)

Results

Notes

# Horse Show Log

Date

Venue

Event

Class

Horse(s)


Results



Notes

# HORSE SHOW LOG

Date

Venue

Event

Class

Horse(s)

Results

Notes

# Horse Show Log

Date

Venue

Event

Class

Horse(s)

Results

Notes

# Horse Show Log

Date

Venue

Event

Class

Horse(s)

Results

Notes

# NOTES

# NOTES

# NOTES

# NOTES

# NOTES

# NOTES

# NOTES

# NOTES

# Notes

# NOTES

# NOTES

# NOTES

# NOTES

# NOTES

# NOTES

# NOTES

# NOTES

# NOTES

# NOTES

# NOTES

# NOTES

# NOTES

# NOTES

# NOTES

# NOTES

# NOTES

# NOTES

# NOTES

# NOTES

# NOTES

# NOTES

# NOTES

# NOTES

# NOTES

# NOTES

# NOTES

# NOTES

# NOTES

# NOTES

# NOTES

# EXPENDITURES LOG

| DATE | ITEM | PRICE |
|---|---|---|
| | | |
| | | |
| | | |
| | | |
| | | |
| | | |
| | | |
| | | |
| | | |
| | | |
| | | |
| | | |
| | | |
| | | |
| | | |
| | | |
| | | |
| | | |

# Expenditures Log

| DATE | ITEM | PRICE |
|------|------|-------|
|  |  |  |
|  |  |  |
|  |  |  |
|  |  |  |
|  |  |  |
|  |  |  |
|  |  |  |
|  |  |  |
|  |  |  |
|  |  |  |
|  |  |  |
|  |  |  |
|  |  |  |
|  |  |  |
|  |  |  |
|  |  |  |
|  |  |  |
|  |  |  |

# EXPENDITURES LOG

| DATE | ITEM | PRICE |
|------|------|-------|
|      |      |       |
|      |      |       |
|      |      |       |
|      |      |       |
|      |      |       |
|      |      |       |
|      |      |       |
|      |      |       |
|      |      |       |
|      |      |       |
|      |      |       |
|      |      |       |
|      |      |       |
|      |      |       |
|      |      |       |
|      |      |       |
|      |      |       |

# Expenditures Log

| DATE | ITEM | PRICE |
|------|------|-------|
|      |      |       |
|      |      |       |
|      |      |       |
|      |      |       |
|      |      |       |
|      |      |       |
|      |      |       |
|      |      |       |
|      |      |       |
|      |      |       |
|      |      |       |
|      |      |       |
|      |      |       |
|      |      |       |
|      |      |       |
|      |      |       |
|      |      |       |

# EXPENDITURES LOG

| DATE | ITEM | PRICE |
|------|------|-------|
|      |      |       |
|      |      |       |
|      |      |       |
|      |      |       |
|      |      |       |
|      |      |       |
|      |      |       |
|      |      |       |
|      |      |       |
|      |      |       |
|      |      |       |
|      |      |       |
|      |      |       |
|      |      |       |
|      |      |       |
|      |      |       |
|      |      |       |

# Expenditures Log

| DATE | ITEM | PRICE |
|------|------|-------|
|      |      |       |
|      |      |       |
|      |      |       |
|      |      |       |
|      |      |       |
|      |      |       |
|      |      |       |
|      |      |       |
|      |      |       |
|      |      |       |
|      |      |       |
|      |      |       |
|      |      |       |
|      |      |       |
|      |      |       |
|      |      |       |
|      |      |       |

# EXPENDITURES LOG

| DATE | ITEM | PRICE |
|------|------|-------|
|      |      |       |
|      |      |       |
|      |      |       |
|      |      |       |
|      |      |       |
|      |      |       |
|      |      |       |
|      |      |       |
|      |      |       |
|      |      |       |
|      |      |       |
|      |      |       |
|      |      |       |
|      |      |       |
|      |      |       |
|      |      |       |
|      |      |       |

# Expenditures Log

| DATE | ITEM | PRICE |
|------|------|-------|
|      |      |       |
|      |      |       |
|      |      |       |
|      |      |       |
|      |      |       |
|      |      |       |
|      |      |       |
|      |      |       |
|      |      |       |
|      |      |       |
|      |      |       |
|      |      |       |
|      |      |       |
|      |      |       |
|      |      |       |
|      |      |       |
|      |      |       |

# EXPENDITURES LOG

| DATE | ITEM | PRICE |
|------|------|-------|
|      |      |       |
|      |      |       |
|      |      |       |
|      |      |       |
|      |      |       |
|      |      |       |
|      |      |       |
|      |      |       |
|      |      |       |
|      |      |       |
|      |      |       |
|      |      |       |
|      |      |       |
|      |      |       |
|      |      |       |
|      |      |       |
|      |      |       |
|      |      |       |

# Expenditures Log

| DATE | ITEM | PRICE |
|------|------|-------|
|      |      |       |
|      |      |       |
|      |      |       |
|      |      |       |
|      |      |       |
|      |      |       |
|      |      |       |
|      |      |       |
|      |      |       |
|      |      |       |
|      |      |       |
|      |      |       |
|      |      |       |
|      |      |       |
|      |      |       |
|      |      |       |
|      |      |       |

# EXPENDITURES LOG

| DATE | ITEM | PRICE |
|------|------|-------|
|      |      |       |
|      |      |       |
|      |      |       |
|      |      |       |
|      |      |       |
|      |      |       |
|      |      |       |
|      |      |       |
|      |      |       |
|      |      |       |
|      |      |       |
|      |      |       |
|      |      |       |
|      |      |       |
|      |      |       |
|      |      |       |
|      |      |       |

# EXPENDITURES LOG

| DATE | ITEM | PRICE |
|------|------|-------|
|      |      |       |
|      |      |       |
|      |      |       |
|      |      |       |
|      |      |       |
|      |      |       |
|      |      |       |
|      |      |       |
|      |      |       |
|      |      |       |
|      |      |       |
|      |      |       |
|      |      |       |
|      |      |       |
|      |      |       |
|      |      |       |
|      |      |       |

# Expenditures Log

| DATE | ITEM | PRICE |
|------|------|-------|
|      |      |       |
|      |      |       |
|      |      |       |
|      |      |       |
|      |      |       |
|      |      |       |
|      |      |       |
|      |      |       |
|      |      |       |
|      |      |       |
|      |      |       |
|      |      |       |
|      |      |       |
|      |      |       |
|      |      |       |
|      |      |       |
|      |      |       |
|      |      |       |

# Expenditures Log

| DATE | ITEM | PRICE |
|------|------|-------|
|      |      |       |
|      |      |       |
|      |      |       |
|      |      |       |
|      |      |       |
|      |      |       |
|      |      |       |
|      |      |       |
|      |      |       |
|      |      |       |
|      |      |       |
|      |      |       |
|      |      |       |
|      |      |       |
|      |      |       |
|      |      |       |
|      |      |       |
|      |      |       |

# EXPENDITURES LOG

| DATE | ITEM | PRICE |
|------|------|-------|
|      |      |       |
|      |      |       |
|      |      |       |
|      |      |       |
|      |      |       |
|      |      |       |
|      |      |       |
|      |      |       |
|      |      |       |
|      |      |       |
|      |      |       |
|      |      |       |
|      |      |       |
|      |      |       |
|      |      |       |
|      |      |       |
|      |      |       |

# EXPENDITURES LOG

| DATE | ITEM | PRICE |
|------|------|-------|
|      |      |       |
|      |      |       |
|      |      |       |
|      |      |       |
|      |      |       |
|      |      |       |
|      |      |       |
|      |      |       |
|      |      |       |
|      |      |       |
|      |      |       |
|      |      |       |
|      |      |       |
|      |      |       |
|      |      |       |
|      |      |       |
|      |      |       |

# Expenditures Log

| DATE | ITEM | PRICE |
|------|------|-------|
|      |      |       |
|      |      |       |
|      |      |       |
|      |      |       |
|      |      |       |
|      |      |       |
|      |      |       |
|      |      |       |
|      |      |       |
|      |      |       |
|      |      |       |
|      |      |       |
|      |      |       |
|      |      |       |
|      |      |       |
|      |      |       |
|      |      |       |

# Expenditures Log

| DATE | ITEM | PRICE |
|------|------|-------|
|      |      |       |
|      |      |       |
|      |      |       |
|      |      |       |
|      |      |       |
|      |      |       |
|      |      |       |
|      |      |       |
|      |      |       |
|      |      |       |
|      |      |       |
|      |      |       |
|      |      |       |
|      |      |       |
|      |      |       |
|      |      |       |

# EXPENDITURES LOG

| DATE | ITEM | PRICE |
|------|------|-------|
|      |      |       |
|      |      |       |
|      |      |       |
|      |      |       |
|      |      |       |
|      |      |       |
|      |      |       |
|      |      |       |
|      |      |       |
|      |      |       |
|      |      |       |
|      |      |       |
|      |      |       |
|      |      |       |
|      |      |       |
|      |      |       |
|      |      |       |

# EXPENDITURES LOG

| DATE | ITEM | PRICE |
|------|------|-------|
|      |      |       |
|      |      |       |
|      |      |       |
|      |      |       |
|      |      |       |
|      |      |       |
|      |      |       |
|      |      |       |
|      |      |       |
|      |      |       |
|      |      |       |
|      |      |       |
|      |      |       |
|      |      |       |
|      |      |       |
|      |      |       |
|      |      |       |
|      |      |       |

Made in the USA
Middletown, DE
14 December 2019

80773916R10068